I AM A SEASON THAT DOES NOT EXIST IN THE WORLD

I Am a Season That Does Not Exist in the World

by Kim Kyung Ju

Translated by Jake Levine

Black Ocean
Boston · Detroit · Chicago

Black Ocean
P.O. Box 52030
Boston, MA 02205
blackocean.org

Cover Art and Design by Andrew Shuta | andrewshuta.com
Book Design by Nikkita Cohoon | nikkita.co

I Am a Season That Does Not Exist in the World is published with the support of the Literature Translation Institute of Korea (LTI Korea).

ISBN 978-1-939568-14-4

Library of Congress Cataloging-in-Publication Data

Names: Kim, Kyung Ju, 1976- | Levine, Jake, 1985- translator.
Title: I am a season that does not exist in the world / Kim Kyung Ju ;
    translated by Jake Levine.
Description: Boston : Black Ocean, [2015] | Includes bibliographical
    references.
Identifiers: LCCN 2015040007 | ISBN 9781939568144 (alk. paper)
Classification: LCC PL994.415.K968 A2 2015 | DDC 895.71/5-dc23
LC record available at http://lccn.loc.gov/2015040007

FIRST EDITION

CONTENTS

I

IF THE FEVER INSIDE IT DRIES OUT, MUSIC RETIRES ITS SOUND

II

ONLY FROM OLD BELLS, THE WATER THAT SILENTLY SPILLS

III
IN THE AIR, UNABLE TO LIE ON THE GROUND, DEAD BIRDS ARE CIRCLING HEAVEN

IV
INTIMACY

I

IF THE FEVER INSIDE IT DRIES OUT,
MUSIC RETIRES ITS SOUND

THE OUTSIDE WORLD

Born without arms, a man who painted only the wind.

Biting the brush in his mouth, the man

pushed undiscoverable winds into the paper he painted.

Although people were unable to discern the shapes of his paint

to distant places, back and forth, his brush strokes

made the gentle sounds of a child breathing.

When he couldn't paint, for several months

he climbed a cliff and opened his mouth.

To find a color nobody had discovered

he descended a dark volcano

deep into the snow, in his eyes, inside the womb

it was there where he left

the two hands that he'd been painting.

THE GANGES IN MY WALKMAN

on lonely days I touch my skin

the music roams the empire of my inner body and yet I wonder whether it lives

the blue campfire in the radio I've smoked since the night I turned 12 and the blurred wind flickering, it picks up white noise and waves it goodbye; so just now, dimming under the moist light of the low lamp, I think of one echo flying to the opposite side of the earth

and heading in the opposite direction, a postcard named the soul that I wait for

I guess tonight is about an impossible sensibility, I remember a certain artist's saying, in this alley buying 20 cigarettes, I might've thought of the Buddha's cold eyes pacing back and forth, not remembering home, leaning against the wall in shivers; and because the Buddha's one eyelash seems to have fallen somewhere, from just the idea, I barely become music

among Buddha's practices I love wandering most; wandering is just so—crouching, one's entire life spent trembling, even on a day that breaks through all the love inside the heart, I wake in the attic where I used to quiver; whenever I think of this my eyes smell of the river for several thousand years the Walkman winds and turns the Ganges in my ears—rising through a tiny crack in the window, the smell of the dreams that dead people in the river are dreaming—it's either that or it's the smell of dreams that died when the dead were alive that climb through each window in this city—in any case, why does this goat tied to the post outside the inn cry all night?

recalling every constellation in the sky, a goat might learn just a single expression for human loneliness; perching from the windowsill of the Baba Guest House, young Buddha bites his bloody finger— gazing down into night inside the black water, there is life when the cries of my body's foreign lands wish to write, and in my eyes, slightly trembling, the tears are a fever

SALT FARM AT NIGHT

dragging like dead men on the river

darkness falls on the salt farm

island shadows are carried on the wind

soaked fish in water

white snow fogging the surface

on an abandoned boat's window, the reflection of the river's
    darkness

a huddle of young seagulls smeared on the cabin floor

for dinner, water peeling off the scales of fish

the collarbone of the clouds reflect the distant light of a house in
    mourning

eyes come to see the ebbing tide blur the salt farm

and at night evaporate to white

as a man tying a stone to his injured horse

sinking it in the river and returning

here is the landscape that wind might have painted

spreading the white sound of water like words from the dead

inside the sea without light, why don't we call that sound the soul?

the sun doesn't step across the water, water spreads into the sun

for many thousands of years watch the bitter taste of the river rolling

the water's internal organs to see

PHAEDO

—about becoming thin

Inside a sea with no name, microbial parasites infest the wall of a cave, slowly eating eyes into an atrophy nobody knows. Really, there the fish without eyes might still be alive, but like eyes or wings, organs vanish—completely—arms and legs are slowly stretched thin like rolling out dough for bread—slimmed, the disturbance of language. This is the story about the absolute pitch that, for 500–600 million years, Cambrian beings have lived. Birds suck their mother's milk, unfurl their wings in the sky and look down into an unknown sea. But do the eyes of those birds peer into that underwater cave and watch time dissipate in the water? For several million kilometers birds fly on the wind. Without people noticing, birds disappear. But who can choose to join them? To get closer to the wind, starting from mom, they discard their eyes. And because these things you all call wings are getting thinner and thinner, little by little I disappear, joining what gradually fades outside this world. On the wall of a cave inside the sea with no name we hang upside down and again, we are returned to a foreign land. For instance, while being hoisted up, stretching their tongues through the net and licking the floor of the deep sea, fish that can't open their eyes make small groans. And isn't that sound for the birds that disappeared from the world? Again, fishermen casting fish without eyes back to the sea. When men first learned the net they became acquainted with the music that lived with the fish. About once every 100 years fish on the bed of the sea raise their eyes to a drop of water falling from a bird taking off the surface, and the fishermen that voyaged for 100 years following the eyes of birds, they watch that same target ripple, inverted on the face of the sea.

On the calm floor, with both eyes closed, know that this is loneliness. The bodies of fisherman gradually thinning because they understand eyes are slowly degenerating outside of humanity. And yet I don't have the fish's knee that spread on the stone for a second. Playing peek-a-boo, sad fish ears. But I have this body and it is thinning, so who can tell if the things that disappear without anybody knowing are gradually coming closer to you. Several months after I vacated a house I returned to find a horse lying in the bath on its stomach. But where did the horse put its legs? Perhaps this story of deformity is for another time.

AURAJI RIVER

Like an ink stick dried to an ink stone the river is frozen.

Now is the time when the dark sounds of water are born unto the wind. Spread across the wind, the darkness inside water. If on such a night they can bare to stand still, people who crawled out their graves crouch down and dip both their hands in the river.

Every night, in order to approach the human soul, how far from earth does light fly? On such a night, hanging upside down from a branch, sleeping birds gnash their black teeth and
regaining consciousness after a long flight, a man quietly shakes the cabin of the plane.

A streak of light arrives from an anonymous star. The duration of that light's life flies into my eyes, and yet I wonder, how long does it take for the life of music to be so alone? A lonely man walks with his eyes closed and, in the middle of the river, the eyes of the lonely man make the sound of the night breathing.

Clinging to the tree on a distant mountain, white icicles slowly gush light like a dwarf star. But a long time ago, from their time to my time, the beasts that turned their backs to the light were frozen by the eyes of wind, so they howl and now, in the middle of the river, inside the water, the spirit that drags dark stones, the spirit that carries your eyes, joining me, that spirit is night.

Water is the sound being slowly pushed outside shadows. If that wind opens, notice the evidence: someone who exits a grave with a feeble face passing you by.

SPRING NIGHT

in a bag, 100 Q-tips

inside a swollen throat, an old doctor
flashes a yellow light

right, yes
in the flock, if just one bird dies
that's shivering right?

yeah, right—
riding a boat shaped like a duck
alone, a floating reservoir

night inside an old medical kit
looks at the dust
on a plastic baggy used for prescribing drugs
and written there, the yellow names and dates—
your name and my name

like the white outline left on the wrist
after a watch is removed

tat-tat-tat, spring rain blurs things

a whole night
birds leftover
inside the body, the slush of rushing pee

DRY ICE

For real, I am a ghost. For the living such loneliness cannot exist.

—Sinking Lotus

There are times when, suddenly
I cannot be reminded of mother's handwriting
and from the window of December
I feel that the time that exists
between myself and home
is critically ill.
Romance is like that.
This life will always be without comfort.

At the alley's end, in the corner shop, I stick my face in the freezer.
Roaming through frozen food, without warning
I touch a piece of dry ice.
Time, frozen over, clings and brands my flesh.
What did this dry ice, coldly alive
and disappearing in a hot dust, finally wish to deny?
During the brief instant my finger touched
did the moment have a higher purity than my desire for desolation
and outlive all the time that has taken root inside my self?
I shudder as if the heat in my being has been completely snatched.
As if exposing all the light in the night sky of the city that lives inside my body
in the alley with mercury eyes, for a moment I shine.
I will die as a martyr in a time I will never live!

Wind like mud between the earth and moon drifts by
and today the air in the sky can't rise—
Frost bitten from door to door
that air slowly flows
      like a ghost.

A FRAGMENT OF PREMONITION

for Ri Ahn

I must speak with a critical lens about twilight as a pattern in my eye—the pattern between what you hold and what grips you.

Between the hollow of an elapsed tree and an alley that lives inside a dead bird is the destiny of wind—the silence that I missed because I met you. And here, where the wind dyed the street with the scent of night's grief and man is the lethargy of time being inked into sorrow—here I will write a word: wind is an orphan.

Between the bicycles I discard and the bicycles I lose, the inner world that we ride is being well ruled. Birds without ears like snow falling—and the white snow dipped in the sea, it injures the sea's color. On that day I endured the snow and brought my love back home.

The cloud hangs a red stomach on the mountain gate. Around that time that belongs to the stars that ache in the key of falling snow, on what dreary rotation do I think of my relationship to the earth?

The sound of water inside falling snow is dark. Because winter is the moment when the wave in my eyes darkens, you stand, and because you stand, the silence fell asleep. That silence might return to its deep abnormality—for when the scales and shadow of the stone meet, it is through a single darkness they wetly relate.

MAGNOLIA

On the floor I lie down and fall asleep. I wake.
For 12 years I've lived on my own.

Life is the spirit's audience
or so I thought.
I only meant to fall in love once, but
in this world, the tree that crawled into a shadow
to live and die alone, like an act of marriage, sogs.
And then suddenly the magnolia blooms.

The magnolia's toes spied on my lovers.
Whenever I move house like a bicycle being carried in the cargo of a train
again, I approach the wind.
Inside the tree's throat, how many spiders
open their mouths and dry out so that
the flowers have a place to pass through?
Not on the outside, but the inside, the burn is my prize.
And then suddenly the magnolia blooms.

Love's teeth wet with red.
because it's burning hot, does the magnolia's shadow cry?

In the tree, see the dead flowers hang by their necks.
Like setting free hostages, the magnolia
quietly releases the petal's stems, again
the shadow is bleeding.

THE NAIL AT NIGHT GRADUALLY DEEPENS

How does that nail stuck in the wall gradually deepen
without anybody realizing it?

When we look from this side
it's just a nail stuck in the wall, but
when we look behind the wall in the middle of the void
even if I live for several centuries
inside of a time that can't be touched, the nail
quietly hangs in the air.

When wind seeps in the wall, is the nail swinging the dimness of empty space
like an extra-marital affair between a tree and its empty branch?

I know the nail at night gradually deepens.
At an old motel
I delivered a pocket stuffed with nails
and in that high motel room I took off my wet body
and twisted until, gently, crawling out my mouth
        one red spider.

I know the secret nails bend into at night.

Nobody really owns the beast they raise
until they learn to cry.

FATHER'S DICKHEAD

In the morning at an empty amusement park on a rollercoaster, while spinning in the air, dad waves.

"Son, what happened to my life..." —Amateur Amplifier

One day my dad's dickhead became smaller than mine.

I don't go with the toy truck or my dad to the bathhouse anymore.
I can't go outside with dad's belt around my waist anymore.
Because I don't live inside dad's pocket
I can't go to the arcade anymore—I'm too old.

Once a week for thirty years dad goes to the bathhouse.
Once a week dad buys a carton of the same brand of THIS smokes that I buy.
Once a week, thinking of the winning numbers to the lotto, dad grins alone.

Once upon a time, while he was napping on a vinyl mat, I saw dad's two yellow balls flop out the sides of his briefs and spill down the floor. After the womb slept with a wide tree and returned, I sprung a yellow leaf. When I sleep father comes near me and like a cricket, he lies down quietly. Suddenly I am awake, shivering—a thought—I am as small as something squeezed out of dad's dick. Is the dickead's fate something that becomes smaller and smaller? No, a dickhead is not like that. When you secretly rub against the skin with fingers like the cockpit of a jet, the dick expands in flames. And yet, although dad's dickhead and my dickhead resemble each other like two trees, one tree rises and one lays flat asleep. I grab one of dad's limp THIS cigarettes and laugh. *DAD, YOU MOTHERFUCKER! WE ARE SAD DICKHEADS!* What's the use of rubbing a dead dickhead? After this thought, I buy a carton of fortified milk, come home, and secretly place the carton next to dad, asleep.

Unfold the front / or / unfold the back.

MUSIC IS THE ONLY THING WE NEED TO TRACE THE SHADOW OF OUR LIVES

Early on, seeped with music, the wind couldn't survive. Although it doesn't leave a relic of itself in some faraway country, they call the place music just passed "air."

The 99th requiem, as soon as it is birthed it gradually begins to erase its landscape. Through its friendship with time, music spends its life as an exile in the human world and then it dies. Early on, dragging their chairs while walking, the boys that pounded stiff drinks in the corner only did so because of a burning suspicion they had about exiling time into a particular piece of music.

Entering the mountain of ice, the first skill all snipers learn is breathing. Breath is that which completely soaks in the self; pulling the trigger by one hundredths, hold your breath. The target cannot participate in the breath that the sniper divides completely into his body—in the sense that a sniper is left defenseless in the musical range of his target, this is one sided and can induce a self-hatred close to love. If you think sometimes a sniper's breath is like music, it means you are watching the invisible breath flying from here to there—while listening to his pulse, which is life's final rhythm, slowly the target receives the sniper's music and crumples into a dreamlike expression. The place music just passed is always like an empty theatre—simple and resolute. Like the moment when the performance ends, the conductor's silence is a great cry.

When she was still a girl, because of vertigo, she'd avoid the first frost like the bird that reaches the coldest place on earth and cries—music no longer makes footnotes to her sadness. In the age when all the busts of people were scary, she lived in the house for a few years. And yet when she made a record, she recorded that none had lived. When she became a young man, he called the twisted face girls to his hole and had to be shy for awhile because the music that played belonged to the girl he used to be.

Greeting the music's rainy season, the habit of shaking the inside of the face. Like gently touching the legs of someone who has a terminal disease, like a girl approaches an abandoned guitar in the alley, places a band-aid on it and tee-hee, on the road that came tearing the placenta inside the womb of music, the boy threw himself down completely. Time will hit him and run. Once a week in the prison across the street a piano rings. *That's the emergency room.* The boy that broke into the empty house to play the piano was caught. He became a man in prison. Philocinema. In the armed forces now, he never returns. On service break he had his coffin made and sent it to the barracks. Sometimes he thinks this pornography, little by little, repatriates him to a fatherland.

SEALED TRANSCENDENTALISM

one stone
fished out the water, one stone
and in that stone, the carved pattern
made by water—
an illusion that time dropped by
we need more time than it takes
to pull one stone from the water, however

one flower
the flower is the ghost of the tree
and the ghost is what the tree sees
so the flower is a ghost until realizing, suddenly, it's a tree
looking at each other's ghosts with a premonition they will both dry out

one pattern
to form the pattern inside the water
how much does the wind need to blather?
inside one wind is carved a pattern
picking up the eyes of people
wind stops by and becomes the yellow shadow
of a time that passed inside the water
at an unknown depth, fingers cut off the hand
turn white on the river floor

and one time
flying beside a ghost carrying the apparition
of the pattern of water shed by a boat
the flickers of fish so pregnant they were about to explode
pulsed next to the shadow of a buoy
recognizing the phantom of the ship, the lighthouse suddenly breathes
    steam and
the wind's habit of hosting funerals turns into a type of music
like wiping off the table with a dishtowel
that boat slides home
and a concept is moored in the beginning of time

WHO RECORDS THE COMPLETE CHRONICLES OF WIND

1.

In a certain sense, during the time the glacier takes wind and freezes it inside itself, several centuries flow by quicky.

The hikers that arrive at the summit, while eating the snow of the snow covered mountain, they say what it is they have to say. *We are now eating the snow that didn't melt for several hundred years—the wind that we are eating, wasn't it imprisoned to this icy world several centuries ago? Screaming at the mountain, we the people who wished to arrive at the sacred life inside the wind, we were a few centuries late* and then, at that moment, an echo returns

life

can't touch this place

where only an echo

gets soaked

Isn't answering with an echo the only way a human can act human in front of the the echo they cast in the wind?

One day, a mirror broke and the wind that lived inside it bloomed into the sky. Afterward, feeling around for my face, a stranger asked if it would be okay if we could all begin to sing.

2.

Wind is a living fossil. Even after disappearing, all living things survive alone and wander. People cry inside their own world, and yet, everything that lives cries inside the wind's world. Then it dies.

when wind blows

birds

fly

into their dreams

If you look into the human pupils of birds, you are wandering in the eyes of a stranger.

And do those stranger's eyes also smile the dim smile of the people who came and went in front of the chronicle of wind?

In a sense, to the wind, speaking lowly and without thinking is about the same as a joke.

WHITE NIGHT

Listening to the sound of water, having the premonition of winter, the insides of birds run deep. Into the smell of the wind, wet birds came and left, and I realized I needed a little more heat in my body. Humans walk along the line of the shore and the water at night rolls up into the color of the skin of a cucumber. Night throws away the wind, night rustles. The smell of the eyes of a beast that lies in the grass spreads over the land. Light takes off its clothes and the bones between reeds grow cold. At dawn clouds rise more transparent than a scream. Our nerves don't flow down the expressway of life like a perfect square. Even if several years pass, if you want to miscarry the heart, it is more effective to burn the moisture of heavy wind than set the grass ablaze. Picking up the burnt shadows of wind along with a few dead dreams, I realize these scars in the grass are not leftover pieces of wind, but the fever I carry inside myself that, little by little, becomes the color of a returning snowstorm. Hanging in every snowflake are particles of wind. What kind of consciousness would place the arch of a burnt foot inside that body? The sky is split with birds like lines in the palm. So what is the question then? I can't find a place to sleep. Until it's filled to the ribs, I watch the sleeping wind pile with snow. I hear the sound of cool water, inside eyes, inside winter fruit.

THE NIGHT SOMEONE GENTLY TAPS ON THE WINDOW

I turn off the light and lie down in my room.
A little later someone taps on the window.
Tonight with no light
what kind of person knocks?
Is there someone who lived here who hasn't yet left?
If the door opens suddenly
I get the feeling someone who is not myself
that lied here for a long time, got up and left.

I think to myself, that's just my neighbor
and lie down motionlessly, however
a bit later on the window
the person that made the tapping
without leaving a name to attach to the sound
disappears silently.

Feeling like I wasn't the first one here
is a lonely thing and
while rearranging the furniture
I find a black fingernail on the floor
that I used to play with.

Someday will I too come back in front of the time I lived
and be a roaming dream?
Here and there stains in this room
might miss whomever left them and

the balloon I released out this window
might be flying in the sky still.
One day before leaving some room
someone wrote on the wall and left
a heavy sentence in the basement of my eyes.
The night brought down a crimson fever
and I, someday, like the ghost that roamed inside myself, long gone
might also wander.

BRED FROM THE EYES OF A WOLF

If you come to my universe, it is dangerous—
I caught you stealing my bread.

At best life is walking about in the blood we own.

One winter, while he clenched his teeth on his mother's teet
the wolf's pupils slowly got fat.
Mom, continually in this life, why are we growing thin?
When you were born, I licked you.
In front of the girl I love, I want to take off my pants.
Because of your pubic hair, you can die—that's life . . .
If it poured snow, I raised my front legs
and nonstop knocked at the door of man
until your father and I shit on the same spot.
To carry you and your sisters here
for thirty years we drooled—meanwhile
to be beside men, dad cut off two of his legs and left.
Mom, my universe groans—it blows.
Every day I am silent. No noise. Not a footstep.
I hover around her window
but you're not allowed to leave blood on her street.
When people look at your blood, the volume of their footsteps turns to low.
So I understand now—when I see the light, I don't rush to it anymore.
Honey, you are not the only beast that wakes
at the sound of clenching teeth.

Darling, when you get older
I want to lose my way with you at my side.

II

ONLY FROM OLD BELLS, THE WATER
THAT SILENTLY SPILLS

EVEN NOW MOM WEARS HER FLOWER PATTERN UNDERWEAR

I went down to my hometown
and while hanging laundry I discovered the truth—
even now, mom wears her flower pattern underwear.
Snow falls in the market on the cart
where as a kid I stood next to mom
juridiciously selecting our family's underwear.
Like a gigantic ass, the sky unfurled, and into it
the voice burnt in the megaphone selling panties flew away.
Inside the sky mom tried to rub a pair of clouds
from the panties onto her cheek.
The fingers reddened the lining of the flowers into a blur
of the girl my mother still wants to be.
Today that disappeared pattern rouged my face.
As mom proved in her time, life is lived moment by moment
by putting on panties and beginning again.
No matter how many people touch them
the panties stay fresh.
Despite all the touching
the flowers never rot.
The snowflakes burst from eyes get close
to the panties blooming one by one on the line
and blur their flowers.
From the inside of wrinkled buds, drip drip, water spills.

A pair of shy, old panties inside the drawer—
their whole life spent beside snowball sized mothballs
and sunlight, fresh, rare and clean, cozily coagulating
with the smell of flesh turned blue.

A POSTCARD FROM ORPHEUS

Every night do the thousands of bulbs I constructed in the factory when I was 20 still light? The fortune teller I used to frequent has become a hotel. My brother who worked the graveyard shift for years at the power plant on top of the mountain told me he shaved his pubic hair with a straight razor. In this tragedy, to prevent infection, the chicken sucks its wings. And yet, after stabbing one kid in the abdomen with a knife, the girl that was doing the stabbing stabbed herself. Only the interviewer survived and felt very alone. This hotel is like the dorm Hölderlin and Hegel embraced each other and slept together in. Like the last time, don't steal the cork again. After we split I thought of the cork shop I always went to. You wanted to be a cartoonist, but you became the exorcist that you painted in your eyes instead. Sleeping with your face on *Phenomonology of Mind*, I thought of your face. Did the witch that was chased by people walk into the river? *Hello! I'm a wanted man. And that is like the same thing as keeping my promise to you.* Last night I secretly entered an empty train and played chess with the dead. If I lost the way, I confess that I raised a scaredy beast. If I carry red bricks on my back one floor at a time, my salary is increased by 10 dollars. And on holiday, if I gift wrap a shitton of sesame oil, I can buy you a K-Pop CD. This place is not suitable for a liberalist like you to live. After he introduced me to *The Mountain Inside the Ground*, I could never think life follows us around. On the road do you remember how we met your dad by chance? Begging with his four outstretched hands, he was eating toilet paper. *I carried you on my back and you covered my eyes with two hands,* and remember, you told me the night before you were penetrated, *when I close my eyes, I stop writing musical scores for you.* So I think the ecosystem I raised my horses in is not just like that. The living are born in the dead people's world and the dead are born in the living—it is just like that. After he secretly removed his makeup at night, why didn't Plato know he was a poet? In the afternoon, in the neighborhood around my house, I secretly hung about. Do you know that in the room in my dreams I leave guitar strings like hair, and even when I'm not there the strings keep growing? Detectives put their hands on the sink and giggled while I held your hair and washed your body. If I look for you, someone is there, ready to shoot me into the next life. Do you want to bite my hand? I don't know you yet. Bad! Right before its death, the cockroach that survived on prescription pills pulled out its wings and trembled, afraid. I'm sorry. Last night father passed into a wish you made.

A CLOUD'S LUMINESCENCE

At the end of every night, the cornershop sells a candle.
At the corner a blind masseuse picks a razor blade.
Watching the weather forecast, the owner eats a can past its expiration date.
But the razor has no expiration date.
Too sharp, each one is dangerous.

Ducks biting dead rats enter the sewer hole.
From the sewer, the weather inside a room flows out like sick eyes.
This neighborhood finally turns around.

In a delivery van's cargo, short women browse through fish.
To see fresher fish, a man
changes the last lamp from his pocket and sees

the shadow of the tree elongating little by little.
Night soon will come.
Somewhere else, a child holding a doll without a neck
stares blankly into the sky
and in that same sky, the man looks into the rain
that contains a strange blue smell. *Ah,* the man thinks
that child that used to come around here, he will never return.

But where has the doll's face gone?
Maybe that kid is holding a kitchen knife
cutting the smiling doll's neck off?

The man flicks his cigarette into the gutter.
Birds hatching eggs in the kitchen, little by little, peck apart their eggs.

A cloud's luminescence deepens.

JUST NOW, AGAIN, I SEE THE AIR OF A WHISTLE I BLEW IN MY CHILDHOOD PASS OUTSIDE MY WINDOW

The wind weeps deep inside a cloud. It is raining, so the people with flowing faces separately hug their posessions and enter the used bookstore. One by one they unhappily thrust their books in empty spots. Without anybody realizing it, a worn-out book lies down and spreads out. Fingerprints someone left inside a page ooze into a sentence. In this place, like donkey eyes, does the heart sink into sand? Sealed like the dried petal of a flower, I am looking for a reason or concept inside the fragrance that disappeared. The pages torn from the book begin to come back. If it rains, the book unfolds and, quietly blowing, the damp whistle becomes a swamp. Words look like bug's eyeballs. In a book they sit and melt. Words look like small temples submerged in a whistle. On a road that doesn't exist in this world, the whistle shakes a tree and crosses the water. The whistle comes and flows. Inside the sandstorm overtaking the continent, like a horsefly, somebody's whistle got mixed in. Just now, again, I see the air inside the whistle that I blew in my childhood pass by my window. During the time the uvula of the beast looking at the village was wet like a bat, I hoisted the plant that used to be the youngest kid in my tribe. Over the course of one night, I saw my whistle evolve and cross the highlands. I hide behind dad's back and spy on the reservoir at night. If you are thinking of the chill of the iron stove that fell asleep and woke up inside human time, sister, again I will get off my bike and whistle a whistle that is weaker than yours. In the past, how did the whistle become the burnt smell of an acacia set aflame?

How did the sound that flew out from inside an iron bell become the peeled-off fingernails that return in the middle of the night? Sister, now I am the son-in-law who teaches your daughter to whistle the winds that carry the smell of lonely lips, the winds that visit the banished flowers on the cliff. But really, what is the difference between a bluff and a cliff?

THE RHYTHM OF FALLING SNOW

*Around dusk, falling snow resembles village lights that quietly blow
   in every room.
It looks as if each flake of snow carries around a different piece of time
And now that I have made eye contact with each silent moment
It seems every person misses their own eyes the most.*

January 26, 2004

Abandoned with the lid open
inside the rice pot it snows.
The rhythm of snow
is piling on the bottom of the pot.
Something like the piece of a baby mouse's broken tooth
returns late at night, shivers
and scratches the floor of the pot.
Something like the place a spoon scraped
is splattered across the bottom of a fake silver pot.

I do not know the violent temperature
that could have reversed thousands of times
inside the chronicle of the pot.
Maybe, like pine resin getting fat
when ricewater escapes, gub-gub
it becomes the ancient rhythm of the pot.
If the fever inside it dries out
the music retires its sound

but if it is night, birds also begin to be like the pot
and send down a fever
into the range of sound they cannot touch.

Inside a time feverishly flipped
after the heat of the body is completely erased
a dried life exposes itself.
A spring day is boiling alone in the room
the faint color of rice water.

MY SORROW SUDDENLY BEGAN LIKE A LOVE FOR MOM THAT NEVER EXISTED

Mom sitting in a flower bed blowing a soap bubble. Dad riding my wooden horse. Not returning home. Playing with a bottle cap. We have black shit in our stomach and sleep. Sprinkle a little ramen powder on our palm. Let's eat. Older brother, the floor inside my outer world, that is the thing that I want to be. Sisters at night secretly draw Korean Barbies with big eyes on the white backs of calendars. Riding a bird's ankle, the ant finally topples to the ground. While a satellite passes a forehead that can't sleep on earth, in the distant sky a pupil rolls back into its head with a shiver. From the window of a steeple on a house of worship in the middle-ages, dead soap bubbles once flew in this direction. Inside our armpits, little by little, candlelight began to grow. While skinned mice gather on stairs that tremble and exchange their futures, the kids that are playing ask, *can we complete the sand castle now?* A doll that was accidentally left in the bathtub swam to the river. Not returning home, teeth chattering, the doll grabbed its fingers that fell off and washed them in the water. Princesses at our house grew bigger. Biting cigarettes and taking pictures. When they passed the piano school where the sound of the Brandenburg Concertos flowed, they covered their ears, and like Munch they ran. On the roof frogs with missing uvulas croaked. Mother loosened her hair to the floor, grabbed an eraser, and began to erase the light entering the room. Mom, I will scratch your back. Whatever anybody says, we were raised scratching mother's back. Nightly while giggling, darkness smashes its fingers in the door. While staring at the dark wind's fins being dragged across the ground like a shovel, I open the window and get scared. Everytime I hear the footsteps of a stranger, I can't forget the night when the vision of the scary light rocked into my life. Mom in a nun's habit sitting in a flower bed. Throwing hundreds of safety razors. Hanging out in the cabin of the flipped truck where I used to play, if the dead children return, then really, I am alone. And so, like a love for mom that never existed, my sorrow begins

LIFE SECLUDED

Is time's relationship with existence similar to the one it has with God?
—Levinas *"Le temps et l'autre"*

Inside a yellow recycling box for used clothes
I cram in some rags I used to wear, the blankets I used to use
and I walk away.
Perfectly folded! This is not where we go!
Hang on. Look back. Don't go away!
One day, flowing out the box like a melted window
a sleeve where soy sauce was spilt.
If darkness stacks the inner and outer body of this alley
while some shadow rummages through the box
it might come to understand the warmth of strangers.
Inside a stranger's eyes, the interior world that was borrowed for a second
like a pocket being turned inside-out, again and again
makes one realize that time and so on is something that doesn't belong only to me.
The clothes must hide! The blankets return!
And during the course of this life
even if just for a moment, they can wear my body's warmth.
If I put two hands in the pockets of my pants
and roll over, onto the wall
even if the window covers me, penetrating me deeply with its heat
every piece of cloth the skin touched, every seam, will fray.
I lie down in the canary colored clothes of death
and the space I don't understand
enters my life through borrowed time.

While I become moral in a different life
at night, into a secluded world, strangers begin to compact.

CONCERNING PHENOMONOLOGY OF MIND, THE LAST LETTER SENT FROM HÖLDERLIN TO HEGEL

Before I am dead, will I be able to see my heart just one time?
I know that before death, all one can do is imagine.

1842, November. Hegel to Hölderlin

Hegel, old ships wave in the tide. Snowflakes that had surrendered their weight to the wind wandered in the time of earth and scattered in the churchyard like the breath of God. At the stroke of midnight, the lights from the monastery that humans built on the beach crash on the wind. They disperse. I was finally able to receive your book and letter delivered by the whip of a horse.

When the wind blows, the sea pushes the habitat of clouds down to the forest. However, after the shadow ripped open the tree it lived in from the inside, it jumped out and rolled to the coast of the sea. All the while it did not freeze. For the first time the sea entered the ancient world. Turning inside out, it lived and plowed through its dark humiliation. Since everyone has a pupil like heavy snow, is it possible that the place of my death, closest to my heart, was bereft of the heavy snow inside my eyes? In the mental range that you manifested, right now you are taking the person that exists at the place that is most far from you and making them painful in the place that is most close by. Next to the smooth bank of the Neckar river, inside a drawer, is a picture that we took in a forest of palm trees in June. In the picture, just because the pupils floated in our eyes for a long time, does that make them our own? When God's eyes cure our eyes, it means love. Please trust this. Like hot soup, the horizon is boiling. Hegel, with the energy I have left, tonight, I pull up a chair. I sit and feel that this particular moment is the rolling tide of wood being carved out the inside of a pencil by the blade.

The snow grabs the sound of ringing bells from mid-air and falls down. Every morning the sound of bells in the monastery make the sea flow more fishily. Someday, from my blue hostility toward the world, a strange metaphor will be discovered. If I break the heavy snow as I enter the forest with bare feet, and pick up and eat pieces of the sky that fractioned off into the snow, he who quietly embraces me with his two hands and then disappears, that man must be God. Right now the chairs that you and I stood side by side on the beach are covered with snow. If the seagull is soaking the sky, the blue pupil is the reflection of the light of a sea set ablaze. Where and when can we meet again and die together capturing this mentality? At night when the nuns come and bind my legs and arms and huddle around me and pray, I can see the falcon that lives alone in the tower out the window. That falcon looks a lot like you. Is it still possible for me to visit the island that traveled to you from inside your mind? Will I ever see those wildflowers again? I am dying drinking the nerveless bugs the nuns bring me. Will future generations think of us as aestheticists? Secretly, after pushing the boat to sea, please toss the blood that visited every harbor of my flesh to the whales. All the time, enjoy.

MY NEVER EXISTED BABY CUTTING SUNSHINE WITH A PAIR OF SCISSORS

My never existed baby is cutting the sunshine entering the room.

Because they enter the chopped light, earthworms shit blood.

From time to time I can almost hear the sound of people having a
     sit-in demonstration.

Blast experts started a bonfire on the roof.

My lover grabs her stomach. Understands gravity.

Dead mice pour out a crack in the roof.

Inside eyes floating in a water cup, pubic hair began to sprout.

Because it wants to live, a cat began to lick a dead mouse.

Although I wasn't sick, I drank liquid drugs and my teeth began to melt.

My lover crawls and hides underneath the wardrobe. She spouts
     phosphorescent light.

Don't die! I will cut the sunshine with scissors!

Piece by piece with a pair of scissors, my never existed baby cuts the baby
I never had.

While cutting a dried earthworm

a halo lights the room.

HEAVY SNOW, A RENTAL HOUSE, A LETTER

Isle of the Dead, Oil Painting with Woodcut, 80 x 150cm, 1886

Inside an electric kettle, the roar of waves seethed.
For ages on the sea, news couldn't reach
the deaf boats feeling for the sound of water sent from a faraway land.
The eyes of a school of fish that pass through a deep abyss
are frozen stiff, I thought.
From a distant lighthouse, fire spilt inside this room.
Whenever that happened, I bluely blotted my sea sickness down at the top
    of the page.
Peonies from the quilt rolled over my leg
and the words inside the letters I wrote began to wake.
Private lives that reached a critical state snowed heavily on the side of the page.
Uncompleted letters turned to misery.
Like bottles emptied one by one
because the sad things disappeared, alone
they swung a retired ship out of retirement
and creakily returned.
In their loneliness, more letters were burned.
Like a furnace, the sea began to boil flakes of snow and
if a hand was dipped under a hot tap inside a room
inside the blood in the body, tears were silently bred.
It cannot end like this, I thought—
a mass extermination of inner life.

Are there enough tears left inside the insomniac's body
to descend into a dream?
Although one by one snowflakes disguise the lights of a town
there is love, love, on the side of the planet we can see
here, undiscovered, infinity. We divvy up our shares.

HEAR THE MACKEREL CRY

In a deep place grown flesh is filled to the brim.

If you see the mackerel grill, at first, the mackerel's lips burst. Ahhhh . . . and pop. Sprinkling from the mouth, black fictions flow freely. Like the one bullet in a thousand that weeps in the flame, the ocean pours slowly from the body. On fire, the spine bulges. The spine melts.

We sit around the purple piece of fish we sliced, and that is what we eat. Nothing spared. Not even a bone. After all is cleared, the smell of fish hugs our lips and we fall asleep. Near the sheets I lay my head. Outside the sheets purple lips begin to smack.

While striking the floor with her fin, mom straightens her spine. Mom, please stop dribbling. I can't close my eyes when I think of your spit. Turning on your side, purple bedsores pop. Mom, all the more strange, after the tongue sank it won't come back. While I sprinkle mom's body with water, the tongue finds a word that had a swim through the heart. When life shows me its tail, I cut the body off.

Sunk into the deep, Mom quietly spits purple air. The mackerel is weeping.

ABSENTIA

You could say rain, the same size as a cricket's eyelash, drops. At this moment my soul is like a ring tone from a phone ringing alone inside a room that has long been vacant. Like the sound of a sun shower, or like the pulse of mist falling in a colonized territory, decades ago, feet flogging through the mud of the executioner's square, the chop-chop, hacking through a man's throat, vibrating out the receiver of the phone someone placed on the floor for me to drop. Or if it is not the sound of rainwater spreading from the sky into the whites of the eyes of a man just before he dies, then it could be the ring-ring of a collect call from a friend in Kazakhstan who, after he scraped his knees learning to ride a bike in the snowy tundra, started to cry. In any case, at this very moment, I am a season that does not exist in the world and, without me being there, my soul is time filling an empty room. Hanging like eyeballs, bloodshot raindrops on the window stare at the empty room. The window is a moment of time being placed in this life, but in this life, the window is forever vacant. You could say that all the humanity in me has passed through this place. Inside a blood donation bus, Jesus, wet with rain, roles dry his poor man's sleeve. Lying down and giving blood, he weeps. Jesus says, "I didn't refuse you. You shall be locked within me my whole life." The nurses nearby hide their long tails and say, "Jesus, don't cry. You are too thin. These days people's veins are hard to stick." Throwing his umbrella in the road, Jesus bows his head as he crosses the street. Jesus trembles in the rain. The dead approach and offer Jesus an umbrella. The dead say, "the flood will soon be upon us. To the palace you built, are you trying to return? Did you lose your way?" "I lost my star," says Jesus. Murmuring, the dead say, "as far as sex is concerned, we are about the same." Trying to remember themselves, caught in the rain, to their houses the dead clomp their feet. Losing their minds, they grab and hug the shoes they wore in life and cry. Flowers that bloomed on the mountain melt on the tongue of a rabbit hatched from an egg. On a stone, the sky's vigil falls. Jesus appears outside the window of my bedroom. With his wet nails, he came here to scratch the glass. The blood of Christ pours down his face. I return. Casting life away, the blind man gone to the world of sound. Coming and going, these sentences like braille.

THE NIGHT TEXT MESSAGES FROM THE YOUNG GIRLS AT THE SUGAR FACTORY ROLL BY

Below freezing, my beautiful sugar is melting. Ugh. Like bacteria, floating snowflakes. People come out on the streets and are hit by that snow like "D." They say if lots of snow falls on the body, the body melts, but with soft feet our footsteps quietly die on the roof. We text, "I miss you." Below freezing, even if they say they will give us another blanket, my beautiful sugar is melting. I have to go out to buy birdfeed and so, tonight, below freezing, Do Re Mi Fa Sol La, will the snow rain and sleep fly in through the window? At dawn while watching the snow fall through the small dormitory window, Do Rae Mi Fa So La, like a small charcoal brick, I took one shit. Ugh. Although my beautiful sugar is melting, if the bird freezes to death I must sit on the chair with my eyes open all night. My brother wrote a beautiful poem that said if I am holding the bird that died with its eyes open, I must fly following the floating snow in the eyes of the dead bird. So I stuck myself up a winter tree and that's life. But where are those sentences now? Brother, you flocked, so dig a dog hole in the wall. I have to buy birdfeed, but the new plastic earrings I bought keep falling on the floor. My beautiful sugar is melting, but the bugs that melted to death in the sugar bite their nests and fly away. Every time I carry down, one by one against my breast, the grey panties hung on the roof, where does our sugar fly off to? My calves break off like sugar cubes. Because my beautiful sugar is melting, red snow inside my head flies wrecklessly. Gathering next to the wall, we pass around hard gum we take from our pockets. Although my beautiful sugar is melting, the fins of snowflakes flap around the city. Below freezing, I want to live curling my eyelashes like a mannequin that whispers at night. Ugh. Dreams where I wear pajamas and am packing are dreadful. My sugar is melting, but I am Spearmint. I am Juicy Fruit. Underneath my skirt, gym clothes. Underneath my skirt, gym clothes. Like lowering panties in a cramped bathroom, farewells are not as embarrassing as ideas. Ugh. My beautiful sugar is melting, but I am inside the snowman I made. Will you come and play at my grave? I will give you all the deer I carved from soap.

THE NIGHT'S DESIRE TO PEE

It's been a long time since I returned home. When I reverse my pocket a roly poly falls out. Smelling the wind's dribbled piss

to get my birth certificate, I became the whole night. In the neighborhood office the lights are like time—after several years, with the lights still turned on, on that same journey

because it's been such a long time, dried particles from the stomachs of dust flake off and settle on the floating light . . . just to get my birth certificate.

Just as the times I failed to write down addresses dispersed like the ends of months, my heart became the addresses of the large rusty gates of houses I first saw at night. But was that really me?

Inside the carapace of the roly-poly uncurled on my palm, I smelled the eery smell of the small shade it makes by rolling its body.

Although I remember my old house like a fog, although from the beginning we smelled sad like the inside of ears

like the way I used to watch my sisters from faraway go into the fields to pee like rats with their legs open, this is the world I live in. Irrelevantly alone. Silently if I return home, because of the few roly-polys that rubbed their white stomachs and rolled toward the wall for hundreds of millions of years, then I am the night that wants to search that pocket completely.

LIVER EATING NIGHT

between the sacred and the common

We eat liver. The liver gathered to be eaten.
We eat liver, so tonight
the relationship between our livers deepened.

Liver was presented. 2 bucks, one plate.
No sausage. Just liver.

We eat liver.
The liver of a summer night, one plate.

We eat liver
without water.

Always, like blackening genitals
will we round out into some unkown
horrendous log of shit?

We eat liver.
We gathered so
in whose liver should we make a little nip?
A liver is squeezed
outside the stomach.
I have to punch another hole in my belt.

THE HOUSE WHERE SOMEONE WAS BORN

Because the inside was dark it hid its outsides.
Like gently placing one handful of rice
into the mouth of the dead
clouds arrive.

When it is night
only from old bells, the water that silently spills
is like the cry that completely transcends the self
to the extent that it can no longer be heard.

They say this is the house where someone was born.
When I passed this place, I was not alone.
But who was with me?
Outside, into the wind, the Mognori rings.
The dead approach the wind and lick the gong of the bell.

When dreams swarm on rotted flesh
do fermenting coffins also send the water of the deceased
to flow outside death?
The cremated clouds that gush down as water
become floating epitaphs.
While the last kick of my foot swam across the air
the hole that floated around inside my body
seeped out the hole of my throat.
People who rotted from crying, I see them as wind.

WELL THEORY

The thunder is drying out.
The well is a stain.
Carried by rain, sloshing inside the cloud
shadows fall into the well.
The well grabs and eats a shadow.
The well slightly darkens.
He who burns glass that broke in the yard
and tosses it down the well is a cremator.
The cremator, he's either my father my grandfather or me.
Inside glass burning in the fire
black char feathers upward like a ghost.
Wearing the borrowed flesh it turned inside out
the char resembles a rainy night.
The char is like the soul of glass
going outside for the first and last time.
Like the body of a plant gives birth to the egg of an animal
the well melts and eats the glass. The well develops eyes.

Whenever a gourd is thrown, the well's eyes break with a bang.
If you ask the cremators about the origin of the well
they'll throw liquid fire into your eyes.
Dark shadows in the ground become water in the well.
The first cremator once said,
"Snowflakes fall and sit on the shadow
and wind like a dark box blows
really, as though the well is made of shadows."

Inside every sip of water, the smell of a shadow is mumbling.
Worried that the well's long tongue might climb out
I was scared so
I didn't have the knack for unearthing voices from the ground.
The red eye of a baby chicken who died in my arms, boom
when I threw it toward the bottom
I knew the well clapped its eyelids tight.
And that is about all I know of the nature of the well.

Now it's time for someone to find the well's mother.
Sunlight threads down a dead spider's silken web
and becomes a ghost.
Every night, like after people abandon a child
raise a plant and throw it away
to know the well's depth
the shadow stretches and comes back.
How far? Who is to say?
In what position does the shadow that never touched the well
have to stretch its neck in order to feel its soot?
With only the stain of the wind and shards of light, underage
how did the well survive?
To that place, like a drought, we climb down
and open our black mouths.
From the inside of this orbit of shadows, unknowable,
well lights turn on.
Well lights turn off.

MANHOLE

My friend, the spider threw its house away and left. The spider couldn't help it. Its borders were distressed. Inside time the spider made, it was like a great hunger grew. All the dark episodes when he wanted to fly, soaked with rain, he came here and dried fast. While the spider wandered around dank rooms down the street, whenever he vanished, things like the spoon and chopsticks secretly followed him. Things we don't understand, how do they become so alone? From his inner self, the spider made up his mind to act. A plot, the spider thought, in a basement make an empty room! However, there is one saying that I've never forgot—*mom* . . . Alright, if you ask me about that time, I'm also flying. In the day, as is usual, I watch the spider carve drawings in the wall with a clip of a fingernail. But at night I witness the spider's insurrection. For a long time, while I gaze into the eye of a moth getting its wings bitten off, I question life—from ashes to dust, as life lived on earth, the empty space in the wall, the place I will end up in, is cracking. Even if thousands of years pass into a secret code, the time I have left on this earth will be lost. My life drags as if order in the world never really existed. Save me! Once a spider leaves, it never finds home.

III

IN THE AIR, UNABLE TO LIE ON THE
GROUND, DEAD BIRDS
ARE CIRCLING HEAVEN

THE NIGHT THE CAT LICKS THE GLASS OF A BUTCHER'S WINDOW

Spiders crawl inside the ears
of children sleeping on the street.
Stuck to the window of a midnight butcher's shop, a cat
on its hind legs pawing the glass.
Makeup is peeling on the chopped off faces lying in the trash.
Hooks hung on the wall spread open their vaginas
and drop blood on the face of time.
Inside a fluorescent tube filled with water
bugs lay dead eggs.
Not wearing pants, a reclusive shadow
paces to and fro between chunks of flesh.
The cat stiffens its back. Scowls.
A black tongue begins to lick the meat's neck.
Drooling, while licking intestines
under the street lamp, the hunger of the cat is illuminated
and the humiliation, ecstatic, that the tongue is sucking
stuffs the mouth of a girl turning down the street.

DREAMER

If a bird bites the hair off someone and flies away
at night, that person dreams of flying.
> —from *Natural History*, a book of classic Chinese literature

To cut my long hair
To cut my long hair I leave at night. I jot down in my notebook "there is no place to cut my hair at night." So I want to talk about the slow life of the Green Papua snail that lives in the Bismark Archipelago. Like clouds that float like bubbles of beer, the night is bewitched by its origins. Life flows here from faraway. It wasn't the thunder squeezed from the sky thousands of years ago, but the darkest eye of a tree in the forest that came to visit me.

The place where the beer was ambushed
In order to buy beer, we ambushed the room. Like guerillas we laughed. Like guerillas we bled from the nose. However, like guerillas at the site of an ambush, because we couldn't die, we rose to buy beer. Someone said in front of the window, "I wish to be absolved from the charge of life."

Because we should be talking about "the story of biting lips," a guy wearing black wayfarers folded black paper cranes and placed them on the table. To save the music from sinking inside its own soul, while shivering a little like firewood, again we begin this blue and soggy song. Somewhere in the middle there is "an island we have never been to" that flew towards music. Also, hanging on a Korean persimmon tree like the Chili of some Chilean guy, was a blue ankle. A young man with the lips of a snail secretly hugged the statue of a girl reading a book and took her to his house.

From the water, a string of hair that was pulled out

Dudes, yer all on the same team. For sure, you guys chat it up every night. Are you looking for the basin where you last washed her hair? I'm sorry to tell you, this is not that joint. Just take a peep in the mirror. Look kid, you've got your cigarette in your mouth the wrong way. "Sometimes on vacation, when yer all alone, you've got to flip the cross sideways on the wall. You've got to sharpen the lonely knife." You guys are really all the same. Because the mouths of the birds in my cage don't squawk, again, you'll be here all night.

The last puff of the lime green cigarette

Inevitably I love you today. Because there is no one I love. Today I love you. Because of you, because my eyes are reproducing, inevitably today I love you. Today, inevitably since it's you that I love, behind me a dreadful silence will appear. And yet, I love you. So today is inevitable. Inevitably, today since I love you, maybe my soul will be punished, and yet I dream of an impossible soul like a priest who can't bury the body because he loves the corpse. Because I'm haunted by an apparition, I have no one to love, so inevitably I love you today. Today the wind that has been alive for thousands of years grabs a strand of my hair and flies far away. However, there is no one I love so, inevitably, today I love you.

From all of this, from the end of the lime green cigarette, smoke.

The diver with a guitar slung on his back

In order to get courage, from the window I quietly move toward my bed. "It's raining, but if you are wandering beside the window, then you are making love," is what I wrote down one time in my notebook. I was scared once sooooooooooooooooo my mouth became majorly twisted. I mean, do I really need to leave the house to cut my hair? Even though the wind is blowing like archaeopteryx, first bird known to man, ca-caw ca-caw, on the floor I spread my wings. I type. The divers in the middle of the river with their guitars slung over their shoulders begin to shout their songs again. The smell of music like bubbles rising to the surface of the river. Without exception. On days like today, it doesn't matter where the beaks of birds pick up strings of hair—it's only over my head where they lay.

THE ROOM THAT FLIES TO OUTER SPACE 1

While pushing the room, I go to space.

One by one, the basement rooms inside the ground rise like balllons and fly away. Every night the room that flies to the outside of space is lonely. It says, *Human, I'm hungry.*

Carrying thousands of people's mud huts, the earth flying in space. In that room, to compose the smallest letter on earth, cast the parts of you that are pink in wax. Like embers that wander around, shivering inside the soundness of my mind, the whistle that departs my lips emits the smell of the North Pole. Inside the heart, thousands of square feet stand ready for cultivation. The only way things that don't belong to this world learn to harass this world is by achieving a lonely state.

Loneliness means lying on the floor and listening to the sound of your two eyes. Loneliness is the time it takes to understand the music of your body. Therefore loneliness is the amount of love it takes to understand one life in its entirety. From behind, for his entire life, my dad slept embracing my sick mom. So it's true—no music is listened to with a clear state of mind.

A swing swept off the earth floating in space. During the time human sleep goes to space, I fly out the room. I swing. The technique of suspending myself can only be achieved when someone carries a fever inside their body long enough for an aria in the string of G to flow out my eyes. Drop, drop, while I dust sleep off.

Every night, while pushing out the room, I go to space.

THE ROOM THAT FLIES TO OUTER SPACE 2

the bird and the whistle

When night arrives, birds hanging on the laundry line begin to puke black water.

The stuttering boy goes up to the roof and whistles. Footprints left by birds in the air shatter quietly in the wind. The whistles evacuate. The flocks of sheep inside my soul change the seasons. They evacuate. At night no one can hear the whistles people blew on the roof. The birds that bit them flew away.

On the roof, cotton explodes out the hanging blanket like intestines gored from a sheep. Hundreds of ivory colored bugs burst out the white cotton and blacken into the after-glow of the night sky. Dad, all people have disappeared to the extent of years they have lived. *Shut up! My sheep are weeping.* Dad, the sheep that weep are never mine. They are yours.

Like how on the day spring arrives butterflies wipe away their souls stroke by stroke, I think about how a person disappears to the extent of all their lived years and it makes me cry.

Biting a dead butterfly, a bird flies off to a room on the mountain.

THE ROOM THAT FLIES TO OUTER SPACE 3

play-doh

A cloud listens to the sound of melting snow inside its body.
Wind soaked up by the room is drying quietly.
Like cream squeezed out a tube, my sisters sweep across the floor and sleep.
Beside them, family members molded from play-doh.
We sit around the table and eat.
Eyes made of clay wetly set.
When the lights go out
the light returns to its world without sound.
In that darkness, a play-doh hand drops its spoon and weeps.
Another play-doh hand places its spoon in the hand that dropped its spoon.
A black teardrop raises its head
and stares at the damp shit a rat laid on the window sill.
Because her toes are bending in her sleep
my sister might also be staring at a flock of birds, pitch black.
Like the white smell inside ears, inside hair, inside eyes
a thing that is called a dream
like drying together, huddled inside a single blanket
is the time difference, standing up inside the self.
Kids, if the sadness dries
hold hands, even in class.
A shadow doesn't get sponged into light
until the body cracks in the sun.

THE ROOM THAT FLIES TO OUTER SPACE 4

dry river

He got a new room.

While the silence inside water slowly dries out

he drags shadows from the middle of the air

to the top of the water

in the shape of dusk.

On the dried floor, leftover clumps of grass

shred, riding the wind.

After realizing he is the place from where it was first blown

from the open mouth, departing

a whistle of some stutterer abandoned here.

When night falls, shadows raised from the floor

float into a fog on the face of the water.

On a day like that, through the receiver of the phone

the sound of mom's crying voice resembles a girl you love.

Realizing fog is only what water dreams, he cut down his speech.

Sitting on top of the roof, he watched the water fly away.

After a few golden letters pass, when morning comes

on the islands where they used to dip their bodies in the water

black birds we can't see sit down on the floor and sleep.

Descending wooden stairs into the water

he asked several questions to God.

Then, like netted fish

all the rooms that used to be on the river floor

are suddenly released.

THE ROOM THAT FLIES TO OUTER SPACE 5

for the window, a wish to never go extinct

Window 1

My brother sent a letter. It said he quit painting and became a bus driver. Because their assholes get stuck, people pour hot water from plastic bowls toward the whining dogs in the alley. With a cloth I use to wipe the floor, I wipe the eyes of the dog I raised. Even when it gets dark, the girls with duct tape over their mouths don't stop jumping rope. Everytime they jump, their bodies disappear a little more in the air. Even in the day, bats carrying their babies open their mouths and fly away.

Window 2

The virgin boddhittsava that is stuffed in a tiny room left the house at one time or another. All day long smelling her armpit, the boddhittsava sits on a chair slowly smoking a cigarette. In our neighborhood a rumor got spun about a man coming and going from the window of the boddhittsava's house. Every night from the third story of the house that smells of cotton flower, a paper plane was thrown by a thin wrist that hangs outside the window like a dead branch.

Window 3

At night a young priest presses his face against the window and watches dreams glide into the rooms of humanity. *Father, don't throw me away.* In the middle of the street a nun takes off her panties and stuffs them in the mouth of a dead saint. Every night I hear cries like a cat come from the room with the blue light where the priest and nun go to sleep. I cover my mouth with my hands. I watch my brother's painting. Old moms fog the window with their breath, take their fingers, and draw multiplication tables on the glass. *Hey kids, now I remember my multiplication well. Dad, don't forget me.*

Window 4

Someone presses 114 and asks to be rescued. Someone presses 114 and says I'm really sorry. Someone presses 114 and says a UFO is coming. Someone presses 114 and weeps, one of these days we really have to meet. Someone presses 114 and asks can we talk just a little bit. Someone presses 114 and says we will go our entire lives without seeing each other's face. Someone presses 114 and says in this city that's just the way it is. A mute presses 114 and practices calling his name thousands of times. Someone presses 114 and silently sends a cry without a face. Believing that the phone call is always recorded, to make a fossil of its cries, the window quietly presses 114 into the dark.

Window 5

The definition of extinction is when the sound of a species disappears.

I will not go extinct.

DOLL SYNDROME, THE WHOLE STORY

1. Tickling

I don't get tickled. When I come home I make good jokes. Lately, I've been participating in a web community for people who walk around the street while hugging their dolls. One afternoon, in the days of my childhood when I used to carry around a dried grasshopper, my sister found a naked Barbie, headless. At that time, whenever dad rung mom's neck or twisted the ankle of a butterfly mom had caught, the bugs that buggled about the rice in their pot moved their lives to the stuffing inside the blanket. My sister grabbed her Barbie and tee-hee, she entered the closet and sneered.

2. The King of Insurance

This month, if she is lucky, mom will become the king of insurance. As king, she will receive the bonus of a jade colored bra. In my old diary it states, "We stood outside the restaurant window until it shut. This happened many times." On a hot summer night marinating spinach, Mom wore only a bra which sagged like a damp poplar leaf and said, "Never look at your customers like they are dicks." Several times, just like that, in front of mom my manhood shrunk. And so, like a cripple right after being born, my trauma began. Every moment in this life has an ulterior motive for me. "Are you going to leave this house again carrying only an ashtray?"

3. Infectious Disease

An infectious disease entered the country and made all the animals inside the house grin like apes. Day in and day out, the only guilt I have is to look back in time. Sometimes, suddenly, when I think there is no one behind my back, I feel most ill at ease. Even now, back there is nothing but a swarm of me. So I think of the time you placed your tiny hands down my clothes and into my back. Meanwhile, in secret, I looked inside the anus of the baby chicken I raised. "I know you too well," is what I said to the self that approached me. Out of nowhere I laughed. One day the bus suddenly stopped. The driver grabbed the back of my neck and dragged me out of the bus.

4. Aphasia

Mom, this guy is the least talkative at our school. When spring arrives, I open the egg of a bulb whose light swelled from neglect. The tongues of bugs that lay inside came out with a crash. Dad crawled inside my sick mom like an inchworm. A squeak snuck out between the teeth. Sisters (who increased by one person in the meantime) while I covered your eyes, did we laugh or did we cry? That spring, barefoot, I walked to the board at the front of the class and solved a problem. Hiding behind the cherry tree, incognito, I slung out my dick.

5. The History of Underwear

Until I became an adult and left the house, my dad and I wore underpants at the same time. No, the way I have to say it is that we shared. The last thing I ever wanted to reveal was this fact—dad is still wearing my underpants. Because I sit here and write about the history of my underwear, finally I am okay. Over and over, making fun of myself, I never get tickled. Outside it's not possible for me to laugh.

SYNOPSIS FOR THE THEREMIN

(in light of its substance and attributes)

1.   The Thing that Dominates the Film

Theremin

In 1920 a Russian acoustical phycisist named Theremin invented an electronic instrument. That's why we call the theremin the theremin. From the outside it looks like a small box. Through resonance created inside the box, a wave of synchronic sound flows through vertical space, and within that space two hands swivel and music is jutted out. From their appearance, the player looks like a mime or sorcerer. The tone of the song is dreamlike and sad. Unlike all other instruments, no part of the human body touches the machine. Into the order of empty space two hands enter and, while forming a new order, they compose music. This instrument is incredibly hard to learn. It is presumed that only 30 or so people in the world are proficient at playing it. Like a biological species, these people are almost extinct. The sound of the theremin was upgraded into a synthesizer. For a scene in a movie Hitchcock once used a theremin for a variation of a song, not for the theremin's original sound. Because of the depth of his ear for sound, Theremin (the inventor) was kidnapped by the KGB and forced to listen to wiretaps for the remainder of his life. Then, after several years, he suddenly appeared with aphasia in New York City. There he died from a blockage of the heart. So, in the play, it is important for the instrument to look like a thing that has its own life. (This explanation is a fact.)

2. Character Description
   Ahn In-Hee: (Male) 30
   Occupation: Piano Tuner

His existence is simultaneously human and musical. In his previous life he was music, but when he was reborn, he became human. In the past In-Hee was a song composed for the theremin by the Russian composer Anaxagoras. Therefore, in this scene, although In-Hee was reborn from music into a human, he is still a person composed of music.

Song Seo-Leon: (Female) 26
Occupation: Piano Player

Anaxagoras fell in love with the piano player. In this life as well as the last life, she plays piano. In her previous life her name was Sonya (same person).

Anaxagoras: (Male) 48.
Occupation: Man who became a composer after quitting the KGB

After his wife's death, he quit the KGB and became absorbed with making music. He loved his piano player and disciple, Sonya. Also, he created the composition that was the previous life of In-Hee. To awaken the memory of this composition, Anaxagoras is reborn as the music that In-Hee loves most in his present life. Anaxagoras is sober minded, upright, and poised.

Song Ae-Leon
Occupation: Deaf girl. Seo-Leon's older sister

Even though she cannot listen to music, she hears the soul of its sound. While the music is playing, it is necessary for her to look like she is watching music instead of listening to it. When she listens to the soul of music, her eyes become as white as the song's musical range. One day she realizes that In-Hee's soul is composed of music.

3.   Major Motives and Intentions of the Scene (Play)
     New Substance and Attributes of the Connection Between Characters

<substance>

We view the previous and present life in a different light. For instance, the abiogenical reincarnation theory states that people are either born human or as a living organism, but in the Middle Ages the epigenesis theory dictated that people can be born as music and that music can be reborn into humanity. Like Spinoza said, if we can discard teleological and anthropocentric perspectives of the world, we arrive at pure "substance." Because metaphysical ability is born within human consciousness, Kant argued that without end, human reason tries to transcend its nature and reach toward the foundation of experience. He wanted to simply distinguish between the mind and the desire to pursue the metaphysical realm, but that was all. Metaphysics was his habitat, but the architecture he built through reason cannot account for the theremin. In this play I wrote about his failure.

<attributes>

The composer Anaxagoras, in order to create love between himself and a woman, takes the music that he composed and rebirths it as a human in order that the love he missed in his life can become possible in the next one. He assigns his ego to the inside of music, so he lives on. (This is a metonym for Kant's theory of reincarnation.) In other words, with sorcery he sealed himself inside the music, became eternal, and later as music, he is able to love the girl he loved when he was still a man.

4. Narrative
    Prologue

    <past>
    The hand that visited the womb

Wrapped around a wood house in bleak Moscow, the fog of war.
Seeped inside a cloud, wind trickles out.
Inside the wind, a window.
Anaxagoras is playing the theremin inside a room
and his eyes are as dark as the heart of a cloud.
Drifting into the order of the theremin, a shady hand begins to grow old.
Little by little, every time it enters the core of the air, the hand dries out.
The flesh that grabs bone furrows and, soaked inside the flesh, the whites of
    the bones are revealed.
Like the end of a sorcerer's spell, the hand that visited and left its music in a
faraway land disappears, bundled in blue smoke.

    <present>
    The music inside music

In-Hee meets Seo-Leon, they enter a relationship, and their love begins. The
two meet as piano tuner and piano player. Now, whenever In-Hee listens
to his most precious and beloved music, like a music within music, like a
music he listens to for the very first time (which is actually the music of the
theremin in his past life), he can't quite remember what it is. Whenever
that music flows, it seems as if the music is calling for another music to be
sung. As the love between In-Hee and Seo-Leon becomes deeper, the music

(that is Anaxogoras) begins to become jealous. While the mysterious triangle between Anaxogars (as music), In-Hee, and Seo-Leon is formed within the atmosphere of music, Seo-Leon's older sister begins to sense the sadness within the future of their relationship.

One day, Seo-Leon's sister Ae-Leon bumps into In-Hee. While they are together, Ae-Leon begins to hum the tune of an unkown music that came from inside In-Hee. In-Hee realizes that the music was composed in Russia, so In-Hee leaves for Moscow with his work. In a Moscow slum, In-Hee first hears the music that wandered inside his memories. Reconstructing his life piece by piece, after coming back to Korea, he treats Seo-Leon with an heir of sadness. So far the story was about the juxtaposition of the past (Russia) and the present (Seoul), but from here, all that is left is the story of the past (from Russia).

<the past revisited>
Passion

The composer Anaxagoras, previously a KGB agent, hears the news of his wife's death while on an espionage mission in Eastern Europe. Because of his wife's death, Anaxagoras began to have doubts about everything. He quit his job and locked himself inside his house to focus on music. His pupil, Sonya, played his compositions on the piano. Because of the pity and love for his wife, he hid his passion even from himself. But now he begins, little by little, to love Sonya. However, Sonya doesn't love Anaxagoras. She just respects him.

Madness

In-Hee reveals to Seo-Leon the secret of his past life. He listens with Seo-Leon to the music that he was in his past life, and like air wandering around them, Anaxagoras becomes the music. Although she has never touched one before, Seo-Leon picks up the theremin. However, because Ae-Leon already knows the scary love of Anaxogoras's madness, she makes a scary plan to liberate them from the soul of the music.

<the time before the past revisited>
Sorcery

A wooden house in bleak Moscow. It's raining outside the window.
Anaxagoras is sitting on the worn sofa as if he is played out.
Opening the door, Sonya enters.
With his eye's filled with clouds, Anaxagoras gets up and says, *I made a new song.*
Instead of going to the piano, as per usual, he puts his hand on the theremin.
For you. Anaxagoras sticks his hand slowly inside the theremin's musical space.
The old hand and the young hand, while stirring the order of time, flow together.

The music approaches Sonya and creates a space within her body.
It is almost as if Anaxagoras lies inside that space like a theme.
Sonya is crying. *What are you doing?*
Can we endure until the end of this life?
Anaxagoras closes his eyes and slowly opens his mouth in the direction of his music.
In the next life, please be born as a human.

89

Pity

[This section is written after Giovanni Pico della Mirandolla's "Oration on the Dignity of Man."]

Adam, we didn't give you a fixed status, unique appearance or special talent. You must choose these as you wish. You have no limitations. Your nature is bent by your will. You decide on your own. I put you in the center so that you can easily see all there is in the world. We didn't make you from the sky or earth, as mortal or immortal. You will enjoy the freedom and the honor of creating your life as you choose. You can either be reborn more humble, as a beast, or you can be reborn as a higher spiritual being.

Because in that life was a love I couldn't achieve, I will wake you in music.

RECALLING TARKOVSKY

My mom cuts our family's hair. Dipping the scissors inside black water, she cuts inside. A bird enters the kitchen and flies into a clay pot. Dad worries about the water people drowned in being carried inside the house by wind, so he shuts the vent. Next to the vent, a foot ekes out its grave. "Mom, next year please construct a storage space." "Son, even if I do, it's not like I can lock you in there." Black hair like spring chestnuts stacking on the newsprint on the floor. "How did your hair get this long?" "Husband, please lift your head." "But keeping my head down is more comfortable for me." However, even in this position, I can hear the sound of eyes being cut in the wind. "Dad, over here!" The blue light radiating out the bodies of dead beasts is freezing in the sky. Dead, the open mouths of winged insects hang like mummies on the windowsill. And yet I wonder—why do the eyes of bugs grow dim in winter? After going outside to discard the hair that he gathered, dad sits under an umbrella on the floor. "Dad, it's not even raining. Why the umbrella?" "Shhh, come close to me. Closer. If you are near here you can enter the eyes of the well." Wrapped in the newspaper underneath the pot, hair crawling, swelling. Tonight like black lilies, one by one the disappeared children are scooped out the reservoir.

TIME FOR DRUNK HORSE TALK

Riding the horses, is it not possible for us to go to the place all music was born?

Tonight I think only of horses, drunk.
Suppressed, the horses break free from sleep so
in order to beat the cold, I feed them drink.
Into the water in the trough, I plop the special sauce.
To handle grisly wind and traverse
the mountain range.
While stroking the horse's back
I gaze at the body of time.
Like cancer patients escaping their rooms at dawn
stuffing their faces in the drinking fountain
with their asses in the air
thirst is a singular image
scarily hurled inside the body.

Blowing bubbles, horses ascend the plateau.
From their eyes I watch red steam rise.
They drank a lot so
my horses start to stagger.
I know that if my grip slips from the horse's whip
they'll get drunk, full-speed
so I lay my horses in the snow.
They place their heads in each other's stomachs
(about types of breathing, there are many of which we can discuss)
and ba-da-boom, like a pounding drum, the beating horse's heart!

Also, resonating inside the stomach of a horse
is the sound of strangers breathing.
Night sky, the age of wind is heard inside the wall of a cave.
This silence that references my name, little by little
like the reading of the words of horses scattered on the floor
is like an image of an alternative body made especially for me.
How many bags did I unpack from my horses back?

Again, the horses begin to cross the Gobi desert covered in snow.
Some gallops I recognize
and some gallops I don't, but
tonight I think only of drunk horses.
From the moment of birth, flying into music
like a plane without wheels
instinctually, like the first flight of my internal world, words
stagger and fall. The horses can't move.
As though they decided to give birth on this exact spot
turning toward consciousness, from their inner depth, horses pull out their dicks.
To what extent is a fragment of premonition not just a sad echo inside the body?

From people, that love was a world locked away.

WHERE IS MY FRIEND'S HOUSE?

It's been over 20 years, so I go to search for my friend at his childhood home. The family of my friend says he left the house 20 years ago and never came back. For all these years, how could I not know? After going to that place to meet my friend, I turned around and bam, 20 more years. Now I wonder, was I ever his friend? In childhood, were we enemies? Has kinship between us ever existed? I, who went to search for my friend after 20 years, became depressed. Me, whose memory of our relationship dims, became a poet. You who stayed when I left, what kind of person did you become? And who am I to ask a person that left twenty years ago a thing like that? After twenty years, what kind of person looks someone up at their old house? For the first twenty years I thought it was our friendship I didn't forget, however, after 20 more years, what is evident is that the thing I didn't forget was me. For twenty years the deep tremors you left when you stayed miscalculated where I came to be. The period of time in which you left your parent's nest slowly crossed over to me like a doubt that arises on days when everything is suspicious. So again and again I ask, where is my friend's house? Where is my friend's house? While the music booms get loud, slowly fade.

HEY GARDEN BALSAM STANDING UNDERNEATH THE FENCE

The day a memo was left on the flower by the baby
oh my love, filled with tears, adieu

The flowers watched an entire season filled with tears. Did I pass this child and flower twenty years ago? Snooping about the fence of my childhood house is the same as asking after the child. The pattern of dark wind that lived inside a concrete well creeps toward the sky. In this alley, the wind that wielded to the smell of flowers writhing inside the well could not disappear. I stick my neck out and look into the well as if a last resort. A dragonfly lies in the garden like a stiff leaf. Like a bird made from mother of pearl that spent its entire life pressed into the armoire, like it began decades ago, the wind surveyable by a wing occurs at the altitude of premonition. However, at what point did those ponds floating in air begin to float over there? Like the sound that leaves the inside of the instrument, from inside the wind, crimson light oozes out. Creases silently appear on the face of the sun. The movement of the flowers is a premonition of a night that can't return. Instead of the absence of a doorplate with a big spike, did the baby thickly inscribe the name of a beautiful ghost on the iron gate? On the night when the knuckles of an aging person lying flat become crunchy, even if you are close, you can't touch the fog jiggling inside wind. Mom, did you see? Just now someone walked over our heads. "Come and sit with your back facing away. Dad's ears got cold like flowerless plants." "Did he carry soap inside his bag because he was ashamed of his skin purpling?" With all its might, the skin setting darkly between me and the baby is now like the hue of a night sparrow following the trickle of water on the wind. "Hey, the baby died a long time ago already. You can't see the same rose twice." In this alley, even during the day, streetlamps that look like bent spoons dimly burn like the eyes of a flower named joys to come. Standing underneath the fence, Garden Balsam, Hey!

CREMATED TEMPLE

A man crawling upside down on the ceiling of the Buddhist temple, laughing.
After burning all of his books
he started to sleep while hugging the back of the statue of Buddha.

**Erected on the island, a temple
that also lives within the island's verse.**

Every night while wiping the hot forehead of the statue of Buddha
little by little the man cuts off his lips with scissors.

**—The island does not confine the width of the sea
but the sea confines the island's depth.**

More red than cornelian cherries, the bloodshot eyes of monks.

**A mother fetches an old man, saying, "This is your child."
"Leave it please. Although I don't eat them so well these days…"**

The female Buddha hugging the child
burnt black, lying on its side.
A forest branded by the wind.
The sound of a carp swimming in a rock.

A torch is thrown from a little monk into the sutra coming out the mouth of the Buddha.

Wobbly, the temple begins to collapse.

THE TREE THAT BECAME A PIANO

#1

At night a man brings a pitcher of water to give the piano something to drink. It is the inertia of the man which believes the flowers inside the piano will bloom.

#2

Girls who bite their nails like boys who bite their nails. For no reason, they separate. A nail with fingers.

#3

A girl goes into her house to steal a piano. The boy and girl hung a birdcage on a piano and sank it into the ocean floor. On the girl's fingers, all throughout the night, the boy suckling.

#4

The piano in the ocean says from its ten holes, "Hug me today." The man with his ten nostrils, throbbing, cries. Here is the inertia of holes where birds can't live.

#5

I believe flowers bloom inside the piano. If it is my misfortune, okay. If it is not your immortality, fine. Tonight I think of the place where the tree that became a piano flowered long ago.

Here a piano divorced from its wood.
Here destiny bewitched, the inertia of goodbye.

THE MOMENT AFTER THE RAIN HITS, WE HUG A RAINBOW AND ENTER A HOTEL WITH AN OLD BATHTUB

The people that excavate old graves, inside darkness
have seen things being dragged into the light.
Carefully, they began to dissect the first scene.

ACT I Soliloquy

After the ebb of the tide, all that remains in the mud
are the feet of crabs unhinged from their husks.
I was holding a candle then, when a film flowed in from the sea.

Act II Ghost

Inside darkness, we held each other's not-fully-developed fingers.
The king doesn't have a twin. If one king is born, one has to die.
One king becomes a man. One king becomes a ghost.
A ghost is the body that has pity for life returning to its time.
To return to itself, looking for its time, the body wanders around.

Act III A Hotel

Man: Bugs look for light because they have floated around the street all day. Just think of me as a bug.
Kim: Okay. There are lots of bugs everywhere.
Man: People have no interest in the wings of bugs.
Kim: Bugs don't call themselves bugs.
Man: Really?
Kim: However, look here. Aren't you waiting for something?
Man: Yeah, I'm waiting.
Kim: You aren't in a sound state of mind.
Man: Every night I slowly crawl through water.
Kim: Weird. My son also used to . . .
Kim: You aren't my son, are you?
Man: That person left home a long time ago.
Kim: Right. It's been a long time since my son went.
Kim: Were you abandoned?
Man: The person you are mentioning is your son.
Kim: Right. That was my son.
Kim: (with his face slowly becoming distorted) Am I laughing?
Man: No. But please don't cry.

Kim: (while adjusting his clothes) I have to get going now.
Kim: But these days I can't even remember the road to my house.

Kim chuckles
The Man also begins to laugh.

Man: (approaching Kim while laughing) Shall I carry you on my back?
Kim: (laughing) Really, can you?
Man: (laughing) Of course.

(Kim climbs on the Man's back)

Kim: (giggling) I'm not too heavy am I?
Man: (giggling) No, you are light.
Kim: (like he is whining) Can you make a sound like an airplane?
Man: Vrooooooooooooooooom Vrooooooooooooom

With Kim on the man's back, they exit the rear of the stage.
Into the stage lighting, fading into darkness, the sound of wind.
The scattering noise of falling leaves.
Splashooo, woooosh, the echo of breaking waves.

Beginning from the floor, water begins to swell.
Slowly, the pattern of water fills the interior like stacks of air.
Like it has been wet for a long time,
If you open a shimmer of water, the river that swallowed a hotel
is filled with light on the floor.
If the stage fills completely with darkness
it seems as though voices raised from deep inside the water are being heard.

Voice: Look. In the air, unable to lie on the ground, dead birds circle heaven.

IV

INTIMACY

I'VE TOUCHED YOUR SLEEPING EYES

the womb

First you unroll the crater of the volcano and begin to paint the air. The shadows that pace around inside the heart of clouds take the color descending through air and the thin, shaky sound of the window of a house standing in a faraway field and dress them both in the night's breath. And then, when night does come, opening their mouths and dying, a number of eery bugs give their bodies to the current of the wind. From the moist towels that appear on the bodies of bugs, which one should we pick to take to the inside of color? At the end of agony, taking the brush gently with your eyes closed, now, slowly, the darkness like a groan begins to paint the bent child, asleep, on a slide made of the dead. As is the case, because I don't want to disturb you, I whisper quietly in your ear, "whenever you paint people, you have a habit of beginning with the eyes."

That was something my parents had to say while they were imagining me before I entered the world. The core of darkness and a pillow lying side by side, feeling each others faces with our hands for the things we painted, I admit, my eyes still have not been born. Before you were born, we as babies spent a great deal of time painting the eyes you never had. And whenever we returned to your insides, more than in your eyes, you spent time inside our eyes. Embrace the dead child. Crawling inside the music of the uvula of a couple having fun is a person you resemble. In that moment you speak the truth—you already were a ghost.

The contour of the inside of water glows on the setting sun. The glow of the sunset is mixing with wind while time becomes transparent. Inside that transparency, the painter is constantly wetting his brush in a blood stain that dyes the wind. You melt dark colors and paint night time on the inside of my eyes. I paint a pile of towels inside the heavy, hard shadows that puddled beneath our feet. Are tears the organs of eyes? The insides of eyes are baggy, so the tears that have no walls in their body let out a laugh. Saying you love me, you touch my baggy fingers and sleep. Even accidentally, your eyes float. Your eyes are born. But, to be completely sure, you must float your eyes to a faraway land and die.

To find a piece of itself that became erased, the wind cries inside your body. Hey, someday you too will meet someone who makes the same sound as you when they cry. Like not being able to distinguish the difference between bulbs of flowers, in what form will we paint my death? Humanity's pattern is the moment you see the beautiful eyes of fish and they become difficult to eat—the pattern of humanity is a person sleeping in the valley, a graveyard for butterflies, the thing that disappeared in the darkness, unexpectedly dull, silence. I must confess that I have quietly felt your eyes while you slept. Strolling slowly through the inside of a cloud, my brush in a comatic state. Crouched in the darkness, if you see a human crawling into my body while piercing your eyes, recognize now, I am that light.

A CITY OF SADNESS

Since I can't be buried with everyone side by side, here I record the rule of my death.

Have you ever whistled at a girl on a rainy street?

No matter how good you whistle, a human is a type of sheep that won't come. Speaking from experience, you shouldn't whistle at your mom. Don't whistle at the battalion commander. Never whistle at the nurse to stop. These are the details of how I arrived here. The feeling of slowly becoming music is something nobody else can know. It's a lonely thing. Lonely people whistle lots. If the sun rises and the book shuts, I go to the corner of the garden filled with trees and, like a milk cow, I slowly munch the grass of thought.

I am in exile. Whether in a memory or the distant future, I am in exile.

If you are exiled from humanity, you can easily become diseased. I know my death will be accompanied by severe agony. I will die here writhing in pain. Huns, Scythians, Magyars, Gokturks, Uyghurs, or Mongols like Turkmen are all nomadic people. All their lives they live in exile. The main principle of their life is to go where they please. Part of the order of their life is to remember the light that fades in the eyes of the beasts they raise. At daybreak many were born. At dawn many died.

In my previous life I was not human. I was music. My favorite music is composed of the man who composed me. In his past life he was a man, but he was reborn as music. Whenever I listen to the sound of that music, I repeat my previous life like I am living this life in the past. So again I slowly become music. This is my story.

Music is also a premonition. The alchemy that composes the self is made of a music you haven't yet heard. However, that music is also the thing that is closest to your being. Just now I had a premonition of a time that flew past my side. Whenever I think these kind of thoughts my mind becomes music, and while I drink the music that is called water in a cup, in a far Spanish field my thought grazes on the hair of a herd of sheep.

Will the moment ever arrive when I can acknowledge my entire being? I said I'm thirsty. While living with you I spoke just 8 times.

The sandfly born on a rainy day only knows a world filled with rain. Then it dies. On a rainy day, as soon as the fetus is born, it is thrown in the sewer thinking to itself that the world is a sewer of death. That's only human. On the side of a hill the mother of the fetus looks into the sky while she washes the blood out her womb in the rain. The sun rises. Ants take the umbilical cord that stretched between the mom and the fetus and haul it into the ground. I pull out my binoculars and closely observe. After the rain, if you put your ear to the moist ground you can hear the Gospel of Luke. I listen to the evening worship of the ants. I skip dinner.

The thing that allowed me to endure this long is a thing I can no longer endure. To not understand these things, an announcement: there is no intimacy between the time I lived and me.

The time I lived was a secret alcohol no one has ever tasted. Easily, I got wasted on that milieu's name.

Childhood is the renaissance of life. If I were a muslim, I would bow to the Mecca called childhood six times a day. When I was a child I almost drowned in the reservoir. In that moment of almost death I experienced many feelings at the same time. Drowning in the middle of the water, I saw the light distancing itself from me. Can you imagine? Afterward, I stopped going to school. Instead I went to the middle of the water and spread out my palms and picked up dead birds and recollected that moment of pleasure, feeling close to death. When I entered middle school I couldn't remember the taste of my mother's milk. At daybreak, to remember, I bit my mother's tits.

My pain doesn't have subtitles. Unreadable.

In all pictures there remains a bit of the air leftover from the time each person lived. Like in any warm greeting a cheerful mold blooms, the facial expression flowing into the photo used for your obituary is the same air you are breathing now. While looking at someone's obituary photo, if you feel remote, it is not because you are feeling the person in the picture, but that the pictured person is feeling you, trying to remember this place. And so this is the place where his effort is delivered, but I wonder, what kind of air will flow in the photo of my obit? With this thought, my two eyes become red air.

From inside the picture I get dizzy looking at myself on the outside.
Time difference. Time lag.

The moment I think I am dead, it is like I can't even remember my face.
Because we need a lot of death, I am walking into an order that even you
cannot see.

The candle in my room burns up all the air in my eyes.

A candle light can't stand in another light.
This is why candle light burns only at night.

I believe there is a planet that shares my birth and death, a planet that shares
the same lifeforce as me. 1976—? That is my ether.

While I masturbate, I age thousands of years.
While I masturbate, I am a sad civilization called myself.

If we warmly embrace and suddenly die, thousands of years will pass and we'll
be fossilized. Our descendants will touch us and feel strange. In its rough and
hard texture the sadness of the fossil cannot be expressed. This is my wrath.
After thousands of years, when people touch us, I will be a stone flowing with
tears. That's the savage custom that exists between us.

The speed of memory is faster than the speed of light.

Breaking up with a lover is like suicide. Like being ripped apart from everything you were accustomed to. The reason you fear the afterlife is that it is absent from everything I love. In a strange place, sleep won't come. Sleeping in a strange place is like one night in hell. Because a person is not different than the life he lived, breaking up is like an act of suicide. My friend Kahn said it like this, sometimes that moment arrives faster than the speed of light.

Wind passes the face of a page and leaves. The eastern wind is reticent. Anxiety is a straightforward expression for the self. Daily I receive an injection like eastbound wind.

Last night I came out the base to exhume a grave with my military friends. When the shovel touched the skull, it reminded me of a camel—a camel that collapsed like sand across the desert. After about 4 kilometers it began to smell human. We grilled a bone we found in the grave and told fortunes. The body belonged to the age of the empire of Un. The body wrote poems. The body was a painter who wandered the world painting cliffs. Nowhere can be found a map that expresses the exile of a dream.

If grave robbing our inner self is what we call a dream, then it is possible that everyone is sentenced to a prison called their dreams. Even though they know it is dangerous, everytime people visit their dreams they erect a tombstone. They bring with them an epitaph called memory, place it in the ground, and it becomes history.

Memory is the second life of humans. Because all memory is handicapped, we must wait. Memory is a thing we cannot possess.

Right now the sky is a pink stream. Like Sunday worship, every evening people in the hospital open their windows and dump a sunset in their heart. Written while staring at sunsets through the bars of the penitentiary window, no poetry is more beautiful than the death row inmate's memoir. That's because it is the music of human death. I once confessed that Beethoven is the sound of music that plays out of the dead. Beethoven didn't compose music. Beethoven was music. What he recorded was only his desperation.

Humans are either born and become ghosts or are born as ghosts who don't know they are dead already. This I believe. The ghost that doesn't know it's a ghost disappears without knowing that it disappeared.

I dedicate my primitivism to music. I want to write a poem that begins like that.

Before their death, a vampire couple whose fate was that they couldn't see the light of day crawled and embraced underneath the sun, shattering to pieces. To see just one fragment of light, all that blood was necessary.

No matter what they say, I've lived thousands of nights.

I was born at night (True) and I was raised at night (True) and I wrote poetry at night (True) so from just this fact, from the earth I must be remote (False) A=A-

You can't see the poet's star from earth. However, you can watch the earth from the poet's star.

My mother's brother stuck a handful of earthworms in his Sprite and chugged it down and said "I'm from Jupiter." Even today, if we go to Baek Hospital in Naju my uncle is still throwing the individually wrapped packets of Asian medicine my great aunt gave him in the sewer saying "These are going to kill me." As soon as my uncle turned 40 he scarily became the kind of person that only devours food. He told me the only thing he learned after he came to earth is whistling. My uncle, who entered Chonnam University's astronomy department ranked #1, was a person that whistled well. When I was a kid, after we watched Robocop 2, I have a memory of us in the bathroom side-by-side peeing together like Robocop.

Every morning when I open my eyes I grab my dry crotch in pain. If I get rid of the suspicion called my dreams, then, in a general sense, I am innocent. There's no reason why I have to be here. While I am having this thought, I walk around the corridor and it's like the end of my life. "Sonuvabitch, did you call your mom?" In my military unit, my beautiful junior # 99-71002665 got his ear exploded after he called his mom to request a visitation. Ever since that day, no matter who he's talking to, he lies.

On a moonlit night while I was sitting on the sill of the dormitory window, an unfathomably beautiful girl who nibbled and ate soap was delivered to the room beside me. That girl turns into a rat every night. When she was discovered in the sewer like a rat no one gave her mouth-to-mouth. Between the white of her revealed waist and the white ankle, a jungle of black hair. Her pants, now soaked, could no longer conceal that atrocity. Her face was egg white and she was shi-shi-shivering. Like a rumor, even the power of her beauty could not overshadow the color and texture of the thick hair on her thighs.

My room is too small to call for more flocks of lamb. My drawers and wardrobe are stuffed with sheep. All my sheep have webbed feet.

I believe that one day if I pop my retina like a cork, thousands of canisters of film will roll out my eyes. Because no light enters the inside of my eyes, this is where the film is alive. Because they are a deep, dark castle, light pains the eyes. In the morning I don't open the curtains. My room is always dark.

I have never played with those who don't fly kites in a sky frozen stiff.

I don't sing with people that know more than 100 religious hymns.

I don't do business with those who have memorized their parent's national registration number.

They are the kind of people that won't fulfill their filial piety.

A person who has masturbated to the fiery prologue of Rilke knows this love is entering the castle of your lover and writing there for your entire life.

It's true—I have never tried to live that way.

As far as I know, my friend Kahn said that in his novel he would use sorcery in order to save his lover. Every day Kahn lived his life like a scream. Poetry is what we called the mistakes we made in our lives spoiled with desperation. It's been a long time since I visited Kahn's yurt. There have been several times after waking in the same room as Kahn that I've wanted to strangle him.

Proof of our lives was that we could feel pain, however, pain was not something that could exonerate us. After we admitted this fact, we felt wonderful. Kahn and I have a habit of sleeping crouched like hermaphrodites. If we wake up under the blanket like the leaf of a cabbage, then together we become SAM. Without crime, reality is a police report we live by writing everyday. Stuck together, side by side, we crouch our heads and file the report. If I say it like this I feel guilty.

Maktoob! Memory of the pyramid, stand firm!! Whatever I am, if I dig wrecklessly I am sure to be buried. If you decipher the entirety of your memory, immediately, you have to escape. Immediately after, the stone will crack. The wall will fall. Because everything will collapse, my spiritual station scares me.

The people exiled inside a time I cannot know send me a floating letter made of wind. On nights when sleep won't come I open the window and under the bed I read the letter that arrives. In the lobby the girl would like to see the calendar. The wind that is the letter that flies inside and inflates the girl's gown, from where does it originate?

Whenthemoonwasfull,alone,thegirldeliveredababyattheentrance
ofthestairs.WhenIquietlyapproachedthegirl,shewassoexhausted
shecouldn'tmove.Becauseitwassodark,shecouldn'trecognizemyface.
Limplyinherhandhungafruitknifethatshecutherumbilicalcord
with.Iwasashadowthatapproached,andsheliedholdingashadowI
haveneverseen.Thebabydidn'tcry.Embracingthebabyinmyarms,
Islowlywalkedtowardmyroom.Foraminuteshestretchedherhand
outtowardsomethingIcouldn'tsee,andmumbledsomethinginthe
Altaiclanguage,thenshequietlybegantotouchmyshadowhanging
inthereflectiononthewall.Insteadofhermother'smilk,Ifedthebab
yitsmother'sblood.Atdawn,thecow'steet.Andfromthebaby'sbody
radiatedthescentoflilac.Toavoidtheeyesofothers,inthemorningI
swallowthebabybyitshead,atnightIvomitthebabyup.AtnightIfeed
thebabywiththeteetofarat.Inthedaytimethebabysleepsinsidethe
caveofmybodyhangingupsidedownlikeabatAtnightIrecitemypoetry
tothebaby.Mybaby'seyesgoblind.WhenmybabygrewupIgivemyba
bythesoulofaseagullandmybabyborrowsthebodyofahorseandrun
stothegreenpastureinsidethecalendar.Beforemybabyleftme,itsaid
mypoetrywasbelowfreezing.IwassadsoItriedtolearnMongolafter
mybabyleft,butsoongaveupaftersnowthatfelloutthecalendarfroze
theroom.

Like a sword that leaves a flash while finding the direct path to the bone, tears
are what melt from the glacier of the self. If you want to be cold, first you have
to learn to be warm when you swim. Because the sword is both hot and cold,
it can glide to a far place. Although the tears that flow out from my body are
warm enough to the cut the mind of a stranger, because the tears that flow
inside my self cut within me, they are cold. Tears are a species of fish rotting
inside the self.

The sky flows like Scholasticism. All clouds are the third wave. The wind is as strong as Bacardi 151. Trees are as quiet as a Romanian legend. The forest is as silent as an out-of-date gynecologist. The fog is illogical, the sun is praxis and the lake is cynical. The pill I have to swallow is Francis Baconish And the existence I haven't experienced is still equal to my future And I pray better better than Hegel And my prayer is more metaphysical than Hegel's prayer And the stone staircase is colder than sergeant Lee who was electrocuted to death in Jinhae harbor in June 1999. God is not allowed to embrace concepts And even though I wasn't born in Copenhagen While listening to music called Copenhagen I am Copenhagen And because I am irrational I can't explain anything I believe in And because I can't explain I write And in order not to explain I cry And what I can't explain will be my inheritance. I am a foreign tongue nobody knows, so those who say they can properly say my name and communicate with me are only deceiving themselves. I was wounded by sorrow and I was tortured by poverty and I was assassinated by religion and I survived by touching sergeant Rim's penis every night. Instead of continuing my life like that, everday I committed suicide by poetry, and I seduced beauty with poetry.

I cut the throat of another mosquito that spispispit in my room. There is a Chinese legend of achieving longevity by eating the brain of a mosquito that I believe in, so I collected the heads of mosquitos inside a bottle and placed it in front of the girl's door. Through the keyhole, I had the feeling that the girl watched my back.

If I die, make sure you dissect my body. As is hearsay, if you cut open my chest, there are millions of people floating in blood.

There are several poems I want to kill.

Because I wrote a very beautiful poem, I want to kill a poem and because all poetry is so beautiful, there is a poem I want to kill. The life of a poet who is sympathetic to shame must become a book, and the book a hospital made of the self.

That is my poem.

All poets are prisoners of war lost by God. However, all prisoners of war are professional prisoners.

The only ability I have is the ability to be different than you. The reason I write "I lost!" is not only because I can't win. The reason I live here is because I am different than you. This is a thing that seems very important to you.

I know that while I sleep, from outside the window thousands of red eyeballs look down at me.

In the night I slept after I exhausted my fingers I understood that the self that completely escaped my body mounted my belly and plucked out my eyes. In order not to be robbed, I developed a habit of not opening my eyes until late in the morning. When the self that completely escaped the body goes back inside, when I feel a river of blue blood flow between the floor and my back, at that exact moment, I open my eyes just barely.

I am a soldier fighting in a war without countries. I know the climax is in July. Because I was born in July, while I listen to the music of July I will die. My will consists of a single line of poetry called "myself" that I wrote on the surface of July. If I die, all the Julys of the world will be buried at sea.

This is how I feel.
Hundreds of miles away, tears flow from the statue of Maria.
Hundreds of miles away, a man hit by a car on the ground slowly closes his eyes.
Hundreds of miles away, air shoots out the tires of a hearse.
In a swamp hundreds of miles away, a zebra slowly enters the alligator's mouth.
On a power line hundreds of miles away, in between the birds, one person sits, burying his head into his wings.
Inside a window hundreds of miles away, at the moment the writer finished writing his book, he let out his final breath.

Hundreds of miles away, the angel of death rides here on the subway and hundreds of miles away, nervously pacing back and forth in the living room, a mom wants to get rid of a visiting son who figured out the truth of his birth. In front of the gate of an alley hundreds of miles away someone like myself hangs about

and today, music is like a play.
One night I dreamt a dream.

In the dream, from a distance, a group carrying a coffin came toward me while I sat next to some lake. However, strange enough, the people carrying the coffin began to enter the cold, blue water of the lake. For sure, if they entered the lake, they would all die. I, while feeling inexplicable horror, shouted "Don't do it!" However, they couldn't hear me. No matter how hard

I screamed, my voice could not pierce through the music that spread out from them like a smell. One by one while they were buried in the water, I suddenly had a realization: the people entering the water that were carrying the coffin all had same face as my own. Well, almost the same. They had my face, but all the eyes were missing pupils. But then, I wondered, in the coffin whose body was laid? I ran and ripped away the flowers covering the coffin. I pulled up the lid. There, laid to rest, was my mom. Like the root of a single tree she lay stiff without voice. Instead of her head, my head rest in the arms of my decapitated mother's corpse. My face had my mother's smile. Outside the lake, a group of people were crying. For the first time in my life I heard myself cry out of a stranger's mouth.

HOWEVER, ONE DAY UNINTENTIONALLY

mf

Let's say you and I lied down together in the same place one time. While stroking your tongue, I opened my eyes, and maybe I pulled beautiful glass beads from my pocket to show you. Like a ship heading overseas at sunset, at the moment a long tether in the water is untied, time is the flow of the ship that was lost in its dock. I entered the window where I died in a foreign country, and, although nobody knows, I should have returned your two eyes.

Behind the scenes, I thought that I could be the boy that picked up and played with dim grains of sand.

Let's say that silent barbarism was you. Let's admit that this language is a name for peeling off the dead skin of life. That this language used to come to watch the void that secretly stared at humans.

The map of wind that the birds abandoned searched for the labyrinth of birds, but at night it broke quietly into pieces. If, toward a single person, the endodermis of time could forge a connection in the direction of one mind, could my humanity become a cry? Don't say the inside of every skin has been answered.

Let's say, one day, accidentally, a ship arrived. Because language is no less than time going inside the body of the physics of humanity, let's write, "You and I lied down together in the same place one time and cried."

NOTES:

Phaedo (p. 8)

In the North Sea there is a legendary fish named Gone whose size, which stretches hundreds of miles, nobody can know exactly. If Gone transforms, it becomes a bird called Boong with a back whose size, stretching for hundreds of miles, nobody can know exactly. When Boong rises up to fly, its wings shut out the sky like a screen made of clouds. Really, when the bird flies a storm is built and the bird, while dipping into the South Sea, dives into a pond in the sky. In the book *SolMun*, Gone is the name of a fish, but in the three books called *Sokyong Sokee Seobyukhee*, the story of Gone was absorbed into the Chinese myth of King Yu. In those books Gone was turned into a demon in order to aggrandize King Yu's myth.

In the book of *JangJa*, the imaginary fish named Gone transforms into the bird Boong in the North Sea. Gone's body stretches a great distance. For how many hundreds of miles, no one knows. Boong's back stretches far. For how many hundreds of miles, no one knows. When Boong flies it rises approximately 22,000 miles and covers the sky like clouds. Escaping the North Sea, the bird is always flying to the South Sea. If the two wings slap the surface of the ocean, a wave develops that is approximately 730 miles long. Yes, and at that time Boong shoots up 22,000 miles. After a journey in flight, after half a year, the bird takes a rest.

Leos Janáek (1854–1928) died while hugging the operatic scores to Bohemian songs like "From the House of the Dead" and "The Diary of One Who Disappeared." These scores are now hidden from the public. Even though he decided to go to St. Augustine monastery as a member of the choir to take care of his poor family, because of his parent's death, abject poverty and hunger, he was not able to learn piano, and so he wandered here and there like an exile learning to make music. However, the successive deaths of many of his family members, especially his beloved daughter Olga, forced him to leave to search for his disappeared son. Sad to the very end, en-route, he caught a cold and died from pneumonia. Because of its difficulty, the public has largely ignored his theoretical work, but I believe it is a kind of poetry.

Arnold Schoenberg (1874–1951). Like fabric, the interwoven and complex melodies of Arnold Schoenberg's compositions are a rude awakening for audiences who have never listened to them before. Skeptical of the world of harmony, Schoenberg wanted to create a freer music, so his compositions are rooted in sonic dissonance and atonalism. Schoenberg's most representative song, "Pierrot Lunaire," was set to the words of a transcendental poem by Albert Giraud. Because the song sounds both like talking and singing at the same time, he called this song "Sprechtstimme," which means "speaking sound."

Anton Von Webern (1833–1945). One night after curfew, while smoking a cigarette outside, Anton Von Webern was shot to death by American military police. Webern, after getting rid of the aristocratic title "Von," secluded himself from society, creating his own artistic world. He received a PhD at the University of Vienna, doing his research in musicology and writing his thesis on the musical consciousness of Heinrich Isaac's Choralis Constantinis. Amongst his compositions there is a song whose length is only nineteen seconds, where each note is like looking through a microscope at a miniature world, where shock and silence revolve in turn. He also wrote the angelic "6 Stücke für Streichquartett," whose tonal arrangement is characterized by passage notes. Most of Webern's compositions are ariettas that are less than a minute in length. To transcend the world of logic in music architecture, he dreamt of a new geometry, and it was like advancing into an eternal world.

Olivier Messiaen (1908-92). When Messiaen was 22 years old he began researching the rhythm of birds, which led to compositions like "Exotic birds." Although he was influenced by exoticism, he opposed French nihilists like Eric Satie, Darius Milhaud, and Max Planck, gradually making collections like "Poemes pour Mi," which portray the conflict between God and modern man. Through his innovations in melody and tempo, reflecting opposite forces like the understandable and the incomprehensible, sympathy and neglect, density and sparseness, sound and silence, clarity and chaos, in the work "The Transfiguration of Our Lord Jesus Christ," he reached a state like the spiritual realm of being delivered from worldly existence.

During War World II Olivier Messiaen was drafted into the French army and was sent to Camp Gernaz as a Nazi prisoner. In the camp he witnessed misery and human death and composed a song titled "Quatuor pour la fin du temps," which depicted the Book of Revelation. Risking his own death, he debuted the song on January 15, 1941.

The House Where Someone Was Born (p. 63)

When the Mognori rings, in the empty space lodged between the interval of different frequencies, a new wavelength of an elongated tone is made and extends for a long duration of time. This is a phenomenon that occurs in Buddhist temples in Asia.

Doll Syndrome, the Whole Story (p. 81)

"I don't get tickled" is a line from one of Osamu Dazai's books.

Cremated Temple (p. 97)

The female Buddha that appears in this poem refers to the Bodhittsava. The spirit of the fetus growing inside the womb is called "fetus spirit" and the female Buddha that follows the heavenly way is called the Bodhittsava.

I've Touched Your Sleeping Eyes (p. 107)

This is the tradition of the natives of a South Pacific island. After marriage they have a habit of not eating beautiful things because they think their partners will leave.

A City of Sadness (p. 109)

A City of Sadness(非情聖市): The phrase was derived from the period of warring states for a cold hearted city. The title comes from the 1989 film by Hou Hsiao-Hsien of the same name.

Maktoob means "it is written/it was written," indicating that something was predestined.

TRANSLATOR'S ACKNOWLEDGEMENTS

This book could not have been possible without the help and support of the following people: Hailji, Baba Kim, Jaewoo Woo, Don Mee Choi, Jung Hi-yeon, Hedgie Choi, Erika Jo Brown, Andrew Shuta, Drew Burk, Dick Siken, Joel Smith, Rimbaud, Radiohead, Janaka Stucky, and Kim Kyung Ju.

I am especially indebted to the hard work of Sangkeun Yu and Carrie Olivia Adams for their helping me complete and edit the manuscript.

Thank you to the editors of the following journals and magazines where poems from this book first appeared: *Asymptote, Asia Literary Review, Boston Review, Black Tongue Review, Circumference, Drunken Boat, Eleven Eleven, Fairy Tale Review, Hayden's Ferry Review, Guernica, Gulf Coast, The Literary Review,* and *Paper Darts.*

And thank you to all the people at the Literature Translation Institute of Korea and the Korean Government Scholarship Program for your generous support.